Under the Southern Cross
Aboriginal Australian Astrology

LLH Media

Introduction: Unveiling Aboriginal Australian Astrology

In the heart of the vast Australian continent, where the skies stretch out in all directions, lies a rich tapestry of knowledge that has connected the Aboriginal people to the cosmos for tens of thousands of years. This knowledge is their unique form of astrology, rooted in the ancient Dreamtime and tied to the land, the stars, and the rhythms of life in this ancient landscape.

Aboriginal Australian Astrology offers a profound window into the world's oldest continuous culture, dating back more than 65,000 years, where the timeless understanding of the stars and celestial bodies plays a pivotal role in spirituality, cultural practices, and daily life. This celestial wisdom, intricately woven into the fabric of their existence, opens a portal to a profound and intricate cosmology, much of which has remained hidden from the wider world.

The purpose of this exploration is to unveil this hidden gem of human wisdom. Aboriginal Australian Astrology is not simply a set of rules for reading the stars; it is a way of life, a spiritual connection, a map to the land and its stories, and a living testament to the enduring relationship between the Aboriginal people and the cosmos. By understanding and appreciating this ancient astrological system, we can bridge cultural divides, deepen our respect for indigenous wisdom, and tap into an extraordinary source of cosmic insights.

In this journey through the skies of Aboriginal Australia, we will uncover the celestial stories that have been passed down through countless generations. We will learn about the Dreamtime, where the first people emerged from the cosmic realms, how they traveled across the land, and how their tracks became the Songlines that crisscross the continent. We will explore the constellations that hold stories of creation, life, and love, and we will encounter the totemic animals that guide the spirits of the departed.

As we delve into Aboriginal Australian Astrology, we will encounter profound insights into the cycles of life, including the movement of the moon, the significance of Venus and Mars, and the vital role of the sun in sustaining the land. We will gain an appreciation for the unique connection between the indigenous people, their environment, and the rhythms of the cosmos.

But this journey is not just an intellectual exploration; it is an opportunity for cultural appreciation and cross-cultural learning. Aboriginal Australian Astrology is a living tradition, and its practices continue to this day, carrying immense cultural and spiritual significance. This book aims to respect and honor that significance while making this ancient wisdom accessible to a global audience.

As we begin our exploration, remember that Aboriginal Australian Astrology is not a stagnant relic of the past but a dynamic and living tradition that continues to evolve and inspire. It is a profound celebration of the interconnectedness of all life and the enduring power of celestial knowledge.

Through the pages of this book, we invite you to embark on this cosmic journey, guided by the wisdom of the world's oldest living culture. The stars have stories to tell, and together we will unveil the celestial wisdom of Aboriginal Australia.

Dreamtime Cosmology: The Foundation of Aboriginal Astronomy

In the heart of Aboriginal Australian culture lies a sacred concept known as the Dreamtime. This fundamental idea is at the core of their cosmology, spirituality, and, by extension, their unique approach to astronomy. Dreamtime, also referred to as the Dreaming or Jukurrpa, is a timeless and spiritual dimension that underlies all of reality. Understanding Dreamtime cosmology is essential to grasp the foundational principles of Aboriginal Australian astrology.

1. **The Dreamtime as Creation**: Dreamtime is the Aboriginal understanding of the creation of the world. In this mythic era, ancestral beings, often depicted as animals or humans, wandered the ancient land, shaping it, giving birth to life, and leaving behind a landscape filled with their stories and footprints.
2. **Cosmic Beginnings**: According to Aboriginal belief, the Dreamtime extends to the cosmic realm. It is during this cosmic Dreamtime that celestial bodies, constellations, and cosmic events were created. These celestial elements are inseparable from the stories of the land and its people.
3. **Spiritual and Cultural Significance**: Dreamtime stories carry immense spiritual and cultural significance for Aboriginal communities. They are not mere myths or legends but represent the ongoing connection between the living, the land, and the cosmos. These stories are passed down through oral traditions, art, song, and dance.
4. **The Songlines**: Within the Dreamtime cosmology are the Songlines or Dreaming tracks. These are paths that crisscross the land and the sky, connecting sacred sites, waterholes, and celestial markers. The Songlines are like a map for navigating the physical and spiritual world, and they are closely linked to the stars.
5. **Stellar Creation Ancestors**: Many constellations in Aboriginal Australian astronomy are associated with specific ancestral beings. These beings are believed to reside in the night sky, guiding and watching over their descendants. For instance, the Emu in the Sky constellation represents the Great Emu Ancestor, and the Orion constellation is associated with the hunter ancestor.
6. **Seasonal Changes**: Aboriginal Australian cultures have a deep understanding of the seasonal changes, which are inextricably linked to the movements of celestial bodies. The changing positions of stars and planets signaled the arrival of seasons, the availability of resources, and the timing of ceremonies.
7. **Lore and Law**: The stories and knowledge derived from the Dreamtime, including celestial lore, are a crucial part of Aboriginal law, ethics, and societal organization. They guide everything from land management to interpersonal relationships.
8. **Living Connection**: Dreamtime is not a distant past but a living, ever-present force. Aboriginal people believe that the actions and ceremonies performed today are linked to the events and beings of the Dreamtime. This is reflected in their practices and rituals, including those related to the stars and celestial events.
9. **Teaching and Learning**: Knowledge of Dreamtime cosmology is passed down through the generations. Elders and knowledgeable community members are responsible for teaching the next generation about the Dreaming stories and their relationship to the land and sky.

Understanding Dreamtime cosmology is pivotal to grasping the celestial knowledge and astronomical practices of Aboriginal Australians. It underscores their holistic view of the world, where the land, the sky, and the people are all interconnected through a timeless web of stories and relationships. These stories are not confined to the past; they continue to shape the present and guide the future, both spiritually and astronomically.

The Celestial Canvas: Stars as Storytellers

In Aboriginal Australian astrology, the night sky is not just a random collection of stars but a celestial canvas filled with stories that have been passed down through generations. The stars, constellations, and celestial events serve as storytellers, carrying the rich narratives of Dreamtime, the ancient and spiritual dimension of their culture. Here, we delve into the significance of the celestial canvas in Aboriginal astrology:

1. The Living Library of Stories:

- Aboriginal Australians view the night sky as a living library of stories, with each star and constellation representing a character or event from the Dreamtime.
- These stories are both instructional and entertaining, teaching important lessons about life, morality, and cultural practices.

2. Celestial Navigation:

- The position and movement of stars guided Aboriginal people in their physical journeys across the land. They used the celestial canvas as a map, indicating directions and points of interest.
- The celestial canvas, in conjunction with terrestrial features, formed Songlines, a network of paths and tracks that traverse the continent.

3. Seasonal Timekeeping:

- The changing positions of stars and constellations were used as a celestial calendar. Seasonal changes in the night sky signaled the arrival of various seasons and the corresponding natural events, like the flowering of certain plants or the migration of specific animals.
- These seasonal markers were essential for determining when to gather food, conduct ceremonies, and engage in specific cultural practices.

4. Ancestral Beings in the Sky:

- Many Aboriginal constellations represent ancestral beings who wandered the land during the Dreamtime and then ascended to the sky, where they continue to watch over their descendants.
- For instance, the Milky Way is often seen as the path of the spirits, and the Emu in the Sky constellation is associated with an ancestral creator spirit.

5. Divine Guidance:

- The celestial canvas provided guidance and insights. Elders and spiritual leaders would interpret celestial events and positions as a means of making decisions or predicting outcomes, much like modern astrology.

6. Rituals and Ceremonies:

- Celestial events played a central role in Aboriginal ceremonies and rituals. For example, the appearance of specific stars or constellations signaled the commencement of certain ceremonies.
- These rituals often included song, dance, and storytelling to honor the Dreamtime narratives represented in the stars.

7. Personal and Cultural Identity:

- The celestial canvas is intimately linked with an individual's identity and their connection to their ancestral roots.
- A person's relationship with the stars can play a significant role in their cultural identity and role within the community.

8. Artistic Expression:

- Aboriginal art frequently incorporates celestial motifs, reflecting the spiritual and cultural importance of the celestial canvas.
- Artistic expression is a way of maintaining and sharing the stories conveyed by the stars.

9. Passing Down Wisdom:

- The celestial canvas serves as a tool for transmitting cultural and spiritual knowledge to younger generations.
- Elders share their insights about the celestial stories and how they connect with cultural practices.

The Celestial Canvas in Aboriginal Australian astrology is more than just a stargazing experience; it is a continuous narrative of the Dreamtime that influences every aspect of their lives. The stars are not just distant cosmic bodies; they are living storytellers, connecting individuals and communities to their ancestral heritage and guiding them in their earthly journey.

Sky Ancestors: The Role of the Constellations

In Aboriginal Australian astrology, the constellations play a vital role as celestial guides and storytellers. These groupings of stars are seen as repositories of knowledge, holding the stories of the Dreamtime and serving as maps for cultural and practical navigation. The constellations are often referred to as "Sky Ancestors" and have profound significance within Aboriginal communities. Here, we explore the central role of the constellations in Aboriginal Australian astrology:

1. **Ancestral Connections:**
   - The constellations represent ancestral beings and their journeys during the Dreamtime. They are seen as manifestations of these ancestors, creating a direct link between the spiritual realm and the physical world.
2. **Navigational Aids:**
   - Constellations, along with terrestrial landmarks, provide guidance for navigation through the vast Australian landscape. They were used as markers to find specific locations, sources of water, and safe paths.
3. **Cultural Timekeeping:**
   - The movement of constellations across the night sky helps determine seasonal changes and influences the timing of cultural events such as ceremonies, migrations, and hunts.
   - Specific constellations rising or setting signaled the beginning or end of certain rituals or activities.
4. **Songlines and Dreaming Tracks:**
   - Constellations are integral to the creation of Songlines or Dreaming Tracks, which are complex pathways that traverse the continent. Each Songline is associated with a particular ancestor or Sky Ancestor constellation.
   - These Dreaming Tracks were both physical and spiritual journeys that allowed knowledge, traditions, and stories to be passed from one community to another.
5. **Cultural Symbolism:**
   - Each constellation has its own unique significance and symbolic meaning within Aboriginal culture. For instance, the Emu in the Sky represents an ancestral being and is associated with creation stories.
   - The patterns of constellations often influence artistic expression and are incorporated into traditional art, reflecting their cultural importance.
6. **Storytellers of the Dreamtime:**
   - Constellations are revered as storytellers, with each star forming a part of the narrative. The movement and positions of stars are used to recount the Dreamtime stories.
   - Elders and spiritual leaders are responsible for passing down these stories and their interpretations to younger generations.
7. **Spiritual Connections:**
   - Sky Ancestors, represented by constellations, are deeply connected to the spiritual lives of Aboriginal people. They are believed to guide, protect, and influence daily decisions.
   - Rituals and ceremonies often involve paying homage to the Sky Ancestors, invoking their guidance and blessings.
8. **Astronomical Knowledge:**
   - Aboriginal communities possess impressive astronomical knowledge, understanding the cyclical nature of celestial events and the consistent positions of constellations.
   - This knowledge enables them to predict seasonal changes and engage in celestial navigation.
9. **Community Bonding:**
   - Constellations foster community bonding. Aboriginal communities gather to observe and discuss the movement of the stars, strengthening their cultural ties and maintaining a shared connection to their ancestors.
10. **Modern Relevance:**

- Aboriginal Australian astrology continues to be a relevant and essential aspect of daily life, cultural preservation, and identity in Indigenous communities. The constellations remain a source of spiritual and practical guidance.

The role of constellations, or Sky Ancestors, in Aboriginal Australian astrology exemplifies the profound connection between the celestial and earthly realms. They are not just patterns of stars but living entities carrying the wisdom and narratives of the Dreamtime, guiding the people through their cultural, spiritual, and practical journeys.

Emu in the Sky: A Celestial Guide

The "Emu in the Sky" is one of the most iconic and recognizable constellations in Aboriginal Australian astrology. This celestial guide is more than just a pattern of stars; it holds profound cultural, spiritual, and practical significance for Indigenous communities. Here, we delve into the mystical world of the "Emu in the Sky" and its role in Aboriginal Australian astrology:

1. **Cultural Significance:**
    - The "Emu in the Sky" is an important cultural symbol for many Aboriginal groups across Australia. It is seen as the emu, a significant creature in Indigenous mythology and everyday life.
2. **Creation Stories:**
    - The constellation is associated with Dreamtime creation stories that narrate the origins of the emu and its role in shaping the landscape. These stories vary among different Indigenous communities but often involve the emu's journey and adventures during the Dreamtime.
3. **Navigational Aid:**
    - Indigenous communities have used the "Emu in the Sky" as a navigational guide. Its rising and setting positions throughout the year are linked to the changing seasons and, consequently, the timing of activities such as hunting and gathering.
4. **Seasonal Marker:**
    - The appearance of the "Emu in the Sky" is a reliable indicator of seasonal changes. Its visibility in the night sky is associated with the arrival of emus, which is a key signal for the timing of the emu egg harvest—a crucial food source.
5. **Mimicry in Art:**
    - Indigenous art often incorporates the "Emu in the Sky" as a recurring motif. The distinct shape of the emu, created by dark dust lanes and the Milky Way, is artistically represented in various forms, including rock paintings and carvings.
6. **Spiritual Guidance:**
    - The constellation is believed to hold spiritual significance, with its presence in the night sky guiding and protecting Aboriginal communities. Rituals and ceremonies may involve invoking the spirit of the emu for guidance and blessings.
7. **Astronomical Knowledge:**

- Aboriginal Australians have extensive astronomical knowledge regarding the "Emu in the Sky" and its relationship with other celestial bodies. This knowledge enables precise tracking of seasons and the emu egg harvest.

8. **Modern Preservation:**
   - The "Emu in the Sky" continues to be a symbol of cultural preservation and identity. Indigenous communities work to pass down the knowledge of the constellation, ensuring its relevance in contemporary Aboriginal life.

9. **Storytelling:**
   - The "Emu in the Sky" serves as a visual storytelling medium. Elders and storytellers recount the associated Dreamtime stories, passing down cultural heritage and knowledge to younger generations.

10. **Harmony with Nature:**
    - The "Emu in the Sky" embodies the deep connection Aboriginal Australians have with their natural environment. It illustrates how celestial observations are intertwined with practical activities, cultural traditions, and ecological awareness.

The "Emu in the Sky" represents a striking example of how celestial objects are integrated into the fabric of Aboriginal Australian culture. It serves as a multi-dimensional guide, offering navigation, cultural identity, storytelling, and spiritual connection. This iconic constellation highlights the intricate relationship between the land, the stars, and the people, illustrating the rich tapestry of Aboriginal Australian astrology.

The Southern Cross: Crux and Its Cultural Significance

The Southern Cross, known scientifically as Crux, is one of the most prominent and recognizable constellations in the Southern Hemisphere, including Australia. In Aboriginal Australian astrology, it holds unique cultural significance, symbolizing not only the celestial realm but also the interconnectedness between the land, the sky, and the people. Let's explore the cultural importance of the Southern Cross in Aboriginal Australian astrology:

1. Ancient Celestial Beacon:

- The Southern Cross has been a prominent feature of the night sky for thousands of years. Indigenous Australians have observed it over generations, incorporating it into their cultural and astronomical knowledge.

2. Navigation and Seasonal Calendar:

- The position and orientation of the Southern Cross change throughout the year. This celestial movement serves as a reliable navigational and seasonal calendar for Aboriginal communities. Its visibility is linked to significant events, such as changes in weather, animal migrations, and plant growth cycles.

3. Sign of the Seasons:

- The Southern Cross is observed as an indicator of seasonal changes, including the approach of the wet or dry seasons. This knowledge informs the timing of activities like hunting, fishing, and gathering.

4. Ceremonial Significance:

- The Southern Cross often plays a role in ceremonies and rituals, where its appearance in the night sky can mark the commencement of sacred events. It may be associated with initiation ceremonies, corroborees, or other cultural observances.

5. Cultural Stories and Songs:

- The Southern Cross features prominently in Dreamtime stories and songs passed down through generations. These stories convey the cultural and spiritual significance of the constellation and its role in the creation of the world.

6. Star Maps in Art:

- Aboriginal art frequently incorporates the Southern Cross as a central element. Its distinctive cross shape is artistically represented in paintings, carvings, and other forms of Indigenous art. These depictions reflect the cultural and spiritual importance of the constellation.

7. Connection to Land and Ancestral Spirits:

- The Southern Cross is considered by many Aboriginal groups to be the footprint of a significant ancestral being, whose journey created the landscape. It is both a celestial map and a direct link to ancestral spirits.

8. Contemporary Cultural Identity:

- The Southern Cross continues to be a symbol of cultural identity for many Indigenous Australians. It represents their connection to the land, their ancestral heritage, and their enduring spiritual beliefs.

9. Preservation of Cultural Knowledge:

- Elders and cultural custodians within Aboriginal communities play a vital role in passing down the knowledge of the Southern Cross to younger generations. This ensures the preservation of their cultural heritage.

10. Integration with Modern Life: - Despite the challenges faced by Indigenous communities, the cultural and celestial knowledge associated with the Southern Cross remains relevant. It underscores the enduring connection between traditional and modern ways of life.

The Southern Cross, or Crux, stands as a symbol of the profound and enduring relationship between Aboriginal Australians and the celestial realm. It is both a practical tool for navigation and a powerful cultural symbol, reflecting the rich tapestry of Aboriginal Australian astrology and its unique connection to the Southern skies.

Skylore of the Elders: Wisdom Passed Down

The indigenous people of Australia have a deep and ancient relationship with the night sky, which they refer to as "Skylore." This profound connection extends beyond simple stargazing and constellations. It encompasses their cultural, spiritual, and practical understanding of the cosmos. The knowledge of the Elders, passed down through generations, is a key aspect of Aboriginal Australian astrology. Let's delve into the significance of Skylore and the wisdom of the Elders in Aboriginal astrology:

1. Ancestral Wisdom:

- Aboriginal astronomy is rooted in the knowledge and wisdom of the Elders, who have carried the celestial teachings from generation to generation. This knowledge is often considered sacred and is an essential part of preserving the cultural heritage of Indigenous communities.

2. Dreamtime Stories:

- Skylore is intricately linked with Dreamtime stories, which are foundational narratives in Aboriginal culture. The night sky serves as a canvas on which these stories are depicted. Each constellation, star, or celestial event has its own corresponding Dreamtime story, connecting the people to their ancient origins.

3. Star Maps and Navigation:

- Elders have an intricate understanding of the stars and their movements, which is crucial for navigation across the vast Australian landscape. They can navigate without compasses, using the positions of stars and constellations as their guides.

4. Seasonal Indicators:

- Aboriginal Elders use celestial events, such as the rising and setting of particular stars or constellations, to determine seasonal changes. These indicators help them plan hunting, gathering, and ceremonial activities in harmony with the natural world.

5. Lunar Knowledge:

- Aboriginal Elders have an acute awareness of lunar phases and their influence on tides, plant growth, and animal behavior. This lunar wisdom is vital for determining the right times for activities like fishing and planting.

6. Cultural Significance:

- The celestial knowledge of the Elders plays a central role in cultural events and rituals. It dictates the timing of ceremonies, corroborees, initiations, and other cultural practices. The Elders ensure that these events align with celestial occurrences.

7. Songlines and Sky Maps:

- Songlines are intricate maps of the land, often mapped onto the night sky. These maps are memorized and sung by Elders to navigate the landscape and recount Dreamtime stories. They serve as both physical and celestial guides.

8. Connection to Ancestral Beings:

- Aboriginal Elders often identify celestial objects, such as stars and planets, as the physical embodiments of their ancestral beings. This connection fosters a profound spiritual and cultural bond with the cosmos.

9. Passing Down Wisdom:

- The role of Elders in Aboriginal communities is to pass down their Skylore wisdom to younger generations. This ensures that the knowledge and customs associated with the night sky continue to thrive.

10. Modern Relevance: - Aboriginal astrology remains relevant in contemporary Australia. The insights from Elders are sought for issues ranging from ecological conservation to land management, demonstrating the ongoing importance of their celestial wisdom.

The Skylore of the Elders in Aboriginal Australian astrology represents a living connection to the cosmos and the land. It's a testament to the enduring cultural strength and profound understanding of the night sky held by Indigenous communities across Australia.

Lunar Insights: Moon Phases and Rituals

The moon has long been a celestial guide and a source of wisdom for the Aboriginal Australians, and their understanding of lunar phases plays a crucial role in their spiritual, cultural, and practical life. Let's delve into the lunar insights, moon phases, and associated rituals of the Aboriginal Australians:

1. Lunar Phases in Aboriginal Cosmology:

- The moon phases hold a significant place in the cosmology of Aboriginal Australians. Each phase is associated with particular energies, meanings, and activities, making the lunar calendar an integral part of their culture.

2. Connection to Dreamtime Stories:

- The moon phases are linked to Dreamtime stories, which are the foundation of Aboriginal spirituality and culture. These stories often explain the creation of the moon and its connection to their ancestral beings.

3. Seasonal and Ecological Significance:

- The moon's phases guide many aspects of Aboriginal life. For example, they use lunar cycles to determine the best times for hunting, gathering, planting, and fishing, aligning their activities with the natural world.

4. New Moon (Waning Moon):

- The new moon represents a time of new beginnings. It's often associated with initiation ceremonies, where young individuals are introduced to their responsibilities within the community. It's also a time for planning and setting intentions.

5. First Quarter Moon:

- This phase is seen as a time of growth and strength. It's often associated with abundance in nature. Aboriginal Australians may hold rituals and gatherings for sharing and celebrating during this phase.

6. Full Moon:

- The full moon is a time of heightened energy and power. It's often associated with healing and cleansing rituals, as well as significant ceremonies and storytelling. Many traditional dances and gatherings are held under the full moon.

7. Last Quarter Moon:

- This phase is seen as a time of reflection and completion. It's often associated with ceremonies for releasing negative energy, making amends, or resolving disputes within the community.

8. Connection to the Tides:

- The lunar phases also influence the tides, which are crucial for coastal Aboriginal communities. They use their knowledge of the moon to determine the best times for fishing and other maritime activities.

9. Ceremonial Activities:

- The moon phases guide the timing of various ceremonies, such as initiations, weddings, and funeral rituals. These events are aligned with the energies of the moon to ensure their success and significance.

10. Spiritual Significance: - The moon is considered a spiritual guide and protector. Aboriginal Australians often engage in meditative and spiritual practices during the different lunar phases to seek guidance, connect with their ancestors, and receive visions.

11. Storytelling and Songlines: - The moon phases play a role in the storytelling traditions of Aboriginal communities. Elders share Dreamtime stories and cultural knowledge during specific lunar phases, ensuring that these traditions are passed down to younger generations.

12. Contemporary Relevance: - The lunar insights of the Aboriginal Australians remain relevant in modern times. Their knowledge of lunar phases continues to guide activities related to agriculture, fishing, and cultural events.

Lunar insights and moon phase rituals in Aboriginal Australian culture exemplify the deep connection between the indigenous people and the natural world. The moon serves as a spiritual guide, a timekeeper, and a source of wisdom, ensuring that their cultural practices and way of life remain deeply intertwined with the cosmos.

Planetary Perspectives: Aboriginal Australian Views on Planets

The Aboriginal Australians have a unique and profound connection to the night sky, including the planets that traverse it. Their views on planets offer a window into their cosmology, spirituality, and culture. Let's explore the Aboriginal Australian perspectives on planets:

1. Cosmic Patterns and Storytelling:

- Planets, like stars, form part of the cosmic pattern in the Aboriginal Australian sky. These celestial bodies are integral to their Dreamtime stories, which are sacred narratives explaining the creation of the world. Each planet often has a role in these stories, which are passed down through oral traditions.

2. Planetary Motion:

- Aboriginal Australians observed the movements of planets in the night sky. While they didn't have telescopes or advanced equipment, they noted the planets' regular patterns and incorporated this knowledge into their cultural and practical activities.

3. Connection to Ancestral Beings:

- Many Aboriginal groups believe that planets are connected to their ancestral beings or totemic spirits. They view the planets as the homes of these powerful entities or as symbols of their influence on Earth. For example, the planet Mars might be associated with a warrior ancestor or guardian spirit.

4. Seasonal and Environmental Indicators:

- The presence of specific planets in the night sky often signals seasonal changes or the availability of particular food sources. For instance, the appearance of a certain planet might mark the beginning of a hunting season, influencing the timing of related ceremonies and activities.

5. Rituals and Ceremonies:

- Planets play a role in the timing of various ceremonies, such as initiation rites, storytelling sessions, and healing rituals. Aboriginal Australians believe that planetary positions can affect the success and significance of these ceremonies.

6. Dreamtime Navigation:

- In some Aboriginal cultures, the positions of planets were used for celestial navigation. Travelers relied on the relative positions of stars and planets to find their way across the land, connecting the terrestrial and celestial realms.

7. Cyclical Significance:

- The cyclical nature of planets' movements is seen as a reflection of the natural world's cycles. Aboriginal Australians often interpret these planetary cycles as metaphors for life, death, and rebirth.

8. Learning and Passing Down Knowledge:

- Aboriginal elders shared their knowledge of the night sky, including the planets, with younger generations. This educational process emphasized the spiritual and cultural significance of planetary observations.

9. Contemporary Relevance:

- Many Aboriginal Australians continue to incorporate planetary perspectives into their lives. For instance, they may consider the positions of planets when making important decisions, interpreting dreams, or engaging in cultural practices.

10. Preservation of Cultural Knowledge: - Efforts are underway to preserve and document the planetary perspectives of different Aboriginal groups. This work helps protect and share this unique astronomical knowledge with future generations.

The Aboriginal Australian views on planets are deeply intertwined with their spiritual beliefs, environmental practices, and cultural heritage. Their understanding of the night sky, including the movements of planets, is a testament to the intricate relationship between Indigenous cultures and the cosmos, emphasizing the importance of preserving these traditions and wisdom.

Venus and Mars: Cosmic Reflections of Relationships

In Aboriginal Australian astrology, the celestial bodies Venus and Mars hold profound significance as they are often associated with various aspects of relationships and human interactions. Here, we delve into the Aboriginal perspectives on Venus and Mars, exploring how these planets are considered cosmic reflections of relationships:

1. Venus: The Planet of Connection:

- Venus, often referred to as the "Morning Star" or "Evening Star," is deeply linked to themes of connection, harmony, and attraction in Aboriginal Australian astrology. Many Aboriginal cultures view Venus as a symbol of relationships and the bonds that tie individuals and communities together.

2. Venus as a Cultural Mirror:

- Aboriginal Australians observe the evening and morning appearances of Venus in the night sky as an indicator of the best times for storytelling and cultural activities. Venus is believed to enhance the power of these traditions, making it an essential cosmic reference point in the preservation and transmission of cultural knowledge.

3. Venus as a Guide for Family and Community Relations:

- Venus sightings are closely watched for guidance on relationships within families and communities. It is often used as a reference for planning family gatherings, weddings, and other social events, as it is thought to promote positive interactions and communication.

4. Mars: The Cosmic Warrior:

- Mars, known as the "Red Planet" due to its distinctive reddish appearance, symbolizes strength, determination, and conflict resolution in Aboriginal Australian astrology. It embodies the qualities of a cosmic warrior who defends and protects.

5. Mars in Ritual and Conflict Resolution:

- Aboriginal communities often refer to Mars when planning rituals, such as initiation ceremonies, where physical and mental strength is required. Mars is also linked to conflict resolution; its appearance can mark times for settling disputes, emphasizing the need for courage and fairness.

6. Venus and Mars as Dual Energies:

- Venus and Mars are seen as complementary cosmic forces. Venus represents the feminine, nurturing, and harmonious aspects of relationships, while Mars embodies the masculine, protective, and assertive qualities. The interplay between these dual energies is considered essential for maintaining balance in personal and community relationships.

7. Gender and Planetary Influences:

- Some Aboriginal groups associate Venus with women and Mars with men. They believe that the positions and movements of these planets influence gender-specific roles and relationships within the community. Observing these cosmic markers can guide decisions related to gender dynamics and responsibilities.

8. The Dance of Venus and Mars:

- Aboriginal Australians observe the cyclical dance of Venus and Mars as a reflection of the ebb and flow of relationships. The periods when these planets are in close conjunction or opposition are viewed as times of significance, influencing decisions related to partnerships, alliances, and family dynamics.

9. Lessons from the Skies:

- Venus and Mars, through their celestial movements, serve as teachers of values and behaviors. They inspire lessons of cooperation, compromise, and unity, reflecting the interconnectedness of all things.

10. Contemporary Relevance: - While these traditional beliefs are deeply rooted in the past, many Aboriginal Australians continue to reference Venus and Mars when navigating contemporary relationships and challenges. These celestial markers remain an important part of their cultural and spiritual identity.

The Aboriginal Australian perspective on Venus and Mars as cosmic reflections of relationships highlights the profound and intricate connections between celestial events and human experiences. These planets serve as guiding lights, both in preserving cultural practices and in navigating the complexities of personal and communal relationships within Aboriginal Australian communities.

The Solar Dreaming: The Sun's Role in Aboriginal Astrology

In Aboriginal Australian astrology, the Sun, often referred to as "The Solar Dreaming," plays a central and sacred role in their cosmology and belief system. The Sun is not merely a celestial body but a symbol of life, creation, and the interconnection of all living beings. Here, we explore the significance and multifaceted aspects of the Sun in Aboriginal Australian astrology:

1. Source of Life and Energy:

- The Sun is universally acknowledged as the source of life on Earth. In Aboriginal culture, it is seen as the life-giver, providing warmth, light, and energy for all living things. It sustains both the physical and spiritual dimensions of life.

2. Connection to Creation:

- Aboriginal Australians believe that the Sun, through its radiant energy and life-giving properties, is connected to the Dreamtime, a sacred period when ancestral beings created the land, animals, and people. The Sun's daily journey across the sky is seen as a reenactment of this creation story.

3. Daily Rhythms and Rituals:

- The Sun's movement throughout the day, from dawn to dusk, influences the timing of daily rituals and activities in Aboriginal communities. For instance, ceremonies, storytelling, and hunting expeditions often align with the Sun's position in the sky.

4. Seasonal Knowledge:

- The Sun's changing position in the sky informs Aboriginal Australians about the seasons, helping them determine the best times for planting, harvesting, and other agricultural activities. It guides their deep understanding of the natural world.

5. Symbol of Enlightenment:

- The Sun is regarded as a symbol of enlightenment, knowledge, and wisdom. It represents the eternal cycle of life, death, and rebirth. Aboriginal people look to the Sun for spiritual guidance and enlightenment.

6. Solar Myths and Legends:

- The Sun is at the heart of numerous Aboriginal myths and legends. These stories often revolve around the journeys of the Sun, which is sometimes depicted as a cosmic being or ancestral figure with a significant impact on the world.

7. Ceremonial Significance:

- The Sun's movements mark key moments in various ceremonies, such as initiations and rites of passage. Its appearance at specific times signals the beginning of sacred rituals and is associated with spiritual transformation.

8. Solar Art and Symbols:

- Aboriginal art often features depictions of the Sun, showcasing its symbolic importance. Circular motifs in paintings and engravings represent the Sun and its spiritual significance.

9. Astronomical Observations:

- Aboriginal Australians have developed an intricate understanding of the Sun's annual path across the sky. Some groups use the Sun's position to mark significant calendar events, equinoxes, and solstices, which are integral to their cultural practices.

10. The Contemporary Role:
- In modern Aboriginal Australian communities, the Sun's significance remains strong. It continues to guide daily life, including the timing of activities and cultural events, demonstrating the enduring relevance of these traditional beliefs.

The Solar Dreaming, symbolized by the Sun, holds a central place in the spiritual and cultural life of Aboriginal Australians. It represents not only the physical source of life but also the essence of their identity, connecting them to the creation stories, ancestral traditions, and the eternal cycle of existence. The Sun's role in Aboriginal astrology underscores the deep reverence and spiritual connection Aboriginal people have with the cosmos and the natural world.

Songlines in the Sky: Celestial Corroborees

In Aboriginal Australian culture, the concept of "Songlines in the Sky" refers to the interconnected web of celestial pathways and stories that traverse the night sky. These Songlines are integral to their cosmology, serving as a celestial map, storytelling tradition, and spiritual connection to their ancestral heritage. The Songlines in the Sky, often referred to as "Celestial Corroborees," are a fascinating aspect of Aboriginal Australian astrology and spirituality.

1. **Cosmic Dreaming:**
   - Songlines in the Sky are intricately connected to the Aboriginal Dreamtime, the spiritual and mythical time when ancestral beings shaped the land and created the cultural foundation. These celestial pathways are regarded as the dreams of the Dreamtime ancestors, reflected in the night sky.
2. **Navigation and Survival:**
   - Aboriginal people have used the Songlines in the Sky for navigation, as they provided guidance for traveling across the vast Australian landscape. By observing the positions of celestial bodies, they could determine directions and time, aiding in hunting, trading, and intertribal travel.
3. **Astronomical Mapping:**
   - The Songlines are a complex system of astronomical mapping, connecting stars, planets, and celestial features with Earthly locations. These stories serve as mnemonic devices for remembering important landmarks, water sources, and sacred sites.
4. **Oral Traditions:**
   - Just as terrestrial Songlines are passed down through oral traditions, the celestial Songlines are conveyed through storytelling. Aboriginal elders share the narratives of these celestial paths with younger generations, ensuring the preservation of cultural knowledge and traditions.
5. **Constellations and Star Clusters:**
   - Songlines often correspond to specific constellations and star clusters, such as the Emu in the Sky, the Seven Sisters (Pleiades), and the Southern Cross. Each of these celestial landmarks is associated with unique stories and holds cultural significance.
6. **Seasonal Calendar:**
   - Songlines are used as a seasonal calendar. The rising and setting of certain stars and constellations mark changes in seasons and signal the right times for activities like planting, hunting, and fishing.
7. **Ritual and Ceremony:**
   - The Songlines in the Sky play a crucial role in ceremonies, corroborees, and rituals. The timing and positioning of celestial bodies guide the timing of these events, deepening their spiritual significance.
8. **Spiritual Connection:**
   - Aboriginal people view the Songlines in the Sky as a spiritual connection to their ancestors and the Dreaming. The stories told through the stars link them to their roots, fostering a strong sense of identity and belonging.
9. **Contemporary Significance:**

- In contemporary Aboriginal communities, Songlines in the Sky continue to hold cultural significance. They remain vital to the preservation of Aboriginal heritage, contributing to the ongoing strength of their cultural practices.

10. **Astrological Insights:**
    - In addition to their cultural and navigational significance, the Songlines in the Sky offer unique astrological insights. Observations of the celestial world are integral to the Aboriginal understanding of cosmic patterns and cycles.

Songlines in the Sky are a captivating testament to the rich cultural and spiritual heritage of Aboriginal Australians. They demonstrate the intricate ways in which Indigenous peoples have intertwined their connection to the land and sky, using celestial bodies as a medium for storytelling, navigation, and the preservation of their sacred traditions. These celestial corroborees reflect the enduring importance of the cosmos in the Aboriginal Australian way of life.

Rituals and Star Ceremonies: Connecting with the Cosmos

The Aboriginal Australians have a deep and profound connection with the night sky, which is reflected in their rituals and star ceremonies. These ceremonies are an integral part of their cultural and spiritual practices, serving as a means of connecting with the cosmos, understanding their place in the universe, and ensuring the well-being of their communities. Below, we delve into the details of these rituals and star ceremonies:

1. **Corroborees and Songlines:**
   - Rituals and star ceremonies are often conducted as part of corroborees, which are gatherings that involve singing, dancing, and storytelling. These ceremonies celebrate the Dreamtime stories related to the stars and constellations, reinforcing the cultural significance of the night sky.
2. **Guidance for Daily Life:**
   - Aboriginal communities have traditionally used the stars to guide their daily activities. They look to the positions of celestial bodies to determine the appropriate times for hunting, gathering, and various tasks. These practices ensure the harmony of their daily lives with the cosmic order.
3. **Seasonal Connection:**
   - Many rituals and star ceremonies are intricately connected to the changing seasons. Aboriginal Australians closely observe the celestial markers that signal the transition from one season to another, ensuring that they are in sync with the natural world for activities like planting, fishing, and hunting.
4. **Initiation Ceremonies:**
   - Initiation ceremonies are vital in Aboriginal cultures. These rituals often involve connecting the initiates with the celestial world, providing them with knowledge about the stars, constellations, and Dreamtime stories associated with them.
5. **Healing and Connection with Ancestors:**
   - Some star ceremonies are performed for healing purposes. They involve connecting with the stars to seek guidance, wisdom, and healing energy. These

ceremonies aim to connect individuals with their ancestors and the cosmic forces that govern their well-being.
6. **Communication with the Spirit World:**
    o Aboriginal Australians believe that the stars are doorways to the spirit world. Rituals and ceremonies are conducted to facilitate communication with ancestral spirits, seek their protection, and ensure the well-being of the community.
7. **Role of Elders:**
    o Rituals and star ceremonies are typically led by Aboriginal elders, who are the custodians of their cultural and astronomical knowledge. The elders pass down their wisdom to younger generations, ensuring the preservation of these traditions.
8. **Singing the Stars:**
    o Singing is a crucial aspect of Aboriginal ceremonies, including star ceremonies. These songs often contain mnemonic devices that help in remembering the Dreamtime stories associated with specific constellations and stars.
9. **Dancing in Cosmic Harmony:**
    o Dance is a central component of many rituals, symbolizing the connection between the terrestrial and celestial realms. Dance patterns often mirror the movement of celestial bodies, reinforcing the relationship between Earth and sky.
10. **Contemporary Significance:**
    o Despite the challenges posed by modernity, many Aboriginal communities continue to perform these rituals and star ceremonies. These practices remain integral to their identity, spirituality, and the preservation of their ancient cultural heritage.

Rituals and star ceremonies are a testament to the enduring connection between the Aboriginal Australians and the cosmos. They embody the spiritual, cultural, and practical dimensions of Aboriginal astronomy, emphasizing the importance of understanding the night sky for navigation, sustenance, and the well-being of the community. These ceremonies continue to be a vibrant and essential part of contemporary Aboriginal Australian culture, reinforcing their connection to the land, the stars, and the wisdom of their ancestors.

Cosmic Timekeeping: Aboriginal Australian Calendar Systems

The Aboriginal Australians have developed intricate calendar systems that are deeply intertwined with their understanding of the celestial realm. These calendar systems not only serve practical purposes, such as tracking seasonal changes for hunting and gathering, but also hold profound spiritual and cultural significance. Here, we discuss these calendars and their connection to astrology:

1. **Lunar and Solar Calendars:**
    o Aboriginal Australians use both lunar and solar calendars. The lunar calendar is based on the phases of the moon and typically consists of 13 months,

reflecting the lunar cycle. The solar calendar, on the other hand, follows the yearly path of the sun and helps in marking the changing of seasons.
2. **Seasonal Markers:**
    - The solar calendar, in particular, is closely linked to the changing of seasons. Specific celestial events, such as the equinoxes and solstices, are important markers for Aboriginal Australians. These events signal transitions in nature, helping them determine the right time for activities like planting, harvesting, and hunting.
3. **Orion's Belt and the Emu in the Sky:**
    - Orion's Belt holds particular importance in many Aboriginal Australian cultures. The three stars in Orion's Belt are often seen as representing three men hunting. This constellation is associated with the Dreamtime story of the "Emu in the Sky," which is linked to the changing of seasons. When the Emu's head rises and becomes visible, it is a sign that emu eggs are ready to be collected, signifying the start of spring.
4. **Dreamtime Stories:**
    - Aboriginal astronomy is closely connected to Dreamtime stories, which are the creation myths and spiritual narratives of Aboriginal cultures. These stories often incorporate celestial elements, including the stars, constellations, and celestial bodies. The movement of stars and celestial events are seen as the ongoing narrative of the Dreamtime stories.
5. **Astronomical Knowledge Transfer:**
    - Elders and custodians of knowledge in Aboriginal communities pass down their understanding of celestial events and seasonal changes to younger generations. This knowledge transfer is crucial for survival in the Australian landscape and helps maintain their connection to the land and stars.
6. **Practical Utility:**
    - The Aboriginal Australian calendars serve practical purposes, allowing them to predict the availability of food sources, understand animal behaviors, and plan ceremonies. This demonstrates how their calendars are both a reflection of their cultural heritage and an essential survival tool.
7. **Harmony with Nature:**
    - These calendars reflect the Aboriginal Australians' deep respect for nature and their understanding of their place in the cosmos. They believe in maintaining a balance between the physical and spiritual realms and harmonizing their actions with celestial events.
8. **Astrological Significance:**
    - While the calendars are not traditional Western astrology systems, they embody a unique form of astrology that emphasizes the connection between celestial events and terrestrial life. These systems guide them in making astrologically informed decisions that are rooted in their cultural traditions.
9. **Contemporary Relevance:**
    - Despite modernization and societal changes, many Aboriginal communities continue to use their calendar systems. They are not only a reminder of their rich cultural heritage but also an affirmation of their enduring connection to the land, the stars, and their ancestors.

In summary, Aboriginal Australian calendar systems are sophisticated tools that blend practicality, spirituality, and astronomy. They offer a unique insight into how indigenous cultures have understood and harmonized with the cosmos for tens of thousands of years.

Their connection to the land, the stars, and their cultural traditions serves as a testament to the enduring significance of these calendar systems in contemporary Aboriginal Australian life.

The Milky Way: A Galactic Serpent of Myth and Legend

The Milky Way holds a special place in the astronomy and mythology of many Aboriginal Australian cultures. It is often referred to as the "Emu in the Sky," a celestial phenomenon that plays a central role in their astrological traditions and Dreamtime stories. Here, we delve into the significance of the Milky Way in Aboriginal astrology:

1. Emu in the Sky:

- The most prevalent interpretation of the Milky Way in Aboriginal astronomy is that it represents a giant emu stretching across the night sky. This cosmic emu is often depicted in Dreamtime stories and artwork. Its head and neck are seen in the southern part of the Milky Way, while its body and legs extend toward the northern part.

2. Seasonal Marker:

- The "Emu in the Sky" serves as a seasonal marker in Aboriginal Australian calendars. When certain sections of the celestial emu become visible at specific times of the year, it signals the beginning of important events, such as emu egg collection, breeding seasons, and the changing of the weather.

3. Connection to Dreamtime Stories:

- The "Emu in the Sky" is deeply rooted in Dreamtime stories, which are the sacred narratives of Aboriginal cultures. These stories explain the creation of the world, the behavior of animals, and the origin of natural features. The celestial emu is often associated with the Dreamtime story of how the emu came to be, linking the cosmic realm with earthly existence.

4. Ethical and Practical Guidance:

- The presence of the Milky Way's emu in the night sky is not just a celestial spectacle; it also serves a practical and ethical purpose. It guides Aboriginal people in their daily lives by signaling when it is time to collect emu eggs, engage in hunting, or perform cultural ceremonies.

5. Rituals and Ceremonies:

- The appearance of the "Emu in the Sky" can trigger specific ceremonies and rituals. These ceremonies are often conducted to honor the emu as a source of food and as an emblem of survival in the harsh Australian outback.

6. Artistic Representation:

- The emu-shaped Milky Way has been a recurring motif in Aboriginal art for centuries. Indigenous artists have depicted the celestial emu in various forms, including paintings, carvings, and engravings. This art not only celebrates the celestial phenomenon but also reinforces the cultural and spiritual connection to the land and the cosmos.

7. Cultural Continuity:

- The recognition of the "Emu in the Sky" in modern times demonstrates the continuity of Aboriginal culture and its connection to the celestial world. Elders continue to share their knowledge of this celestial marker with younger generations, ensuring that traditional practices and beliefs endure.

8. Cosmic Serpent Symbolism:

- The Milky Way's "Emu in the Sky" is often associated with the symbolism of a cosmic serpent. In some Aboriginal cultures, it is seen as a celestial snake or serpent, which reflects their profound understanding of the interconnectedness of all life forms.

In summary, the Milky Way, known as the "Emu in the Sky," is an essential element of Aboriginal Australian astrology and culture. It represents more than just a starry spectacle; it is a celestial guide, a source of cultural identity, and a bridge between the earthly realm and the Dreamtime stories. The rich mythology surrounding the celestial emu is a testament to the deep spiritual and astronomical knowledge of Aboriginal Australians, connecting them to the land, the stars, and their ancient heritage.

Bush Medicine and Celestial Healing: The Healing Power of Stars

In Aboriginal Australian cultures, the interplay between bush medicine and celestial healing is a reflection of their holistic approach to health and well-being. This deep-rooted connection between the natural environment, the cosmos, and human health is a testament to the intricate knowledge passed down through generations. Here, we explore the significance of bush medicine and its celestial ties:

1. Bush Medicine Tradition:

- Bush medicine refers to the traditional healing practices and remedies that have been used by Aboriginal people for thousands of years. These remedies include the use of native plants, herbs, and minerals with potent medicinal properties.

2. Spiritual Connection:

- Aboriginal cultures hold a spiritual belief that the land, its flora, and fauna are interconnected with the spiritual realm. The ancestors, who are believed to have shaped the land and its natural resources during the Dreamtime, are an integral part of this spiritual connection.

3. The Healing Power of Plants:

- The use of native plants for medicinal purposes is a fundamental aspect of bush medicine. Different plants are known for their unique healing properties, ranging from pain relief to the treatment of infections. This knowledge is passed down orally from one generation to the next.

4. Celestial Guidance:

- Aboriginal communities believe that the celestial bodies, including stars, have a direct influence on human life and health. Celestial bodies are considered as markers for specific periods of bush medicine harvest and use. The stars are used as guides to know when particular plants are at their most potent.

5. Seasonal and Lunar Cycles:

- The Aboriginal lunar calendar, often based on the phases of the moon and the positions of certain stars, helps determine the timing of various healing rituals and medicinal plant harvest. Each lunar phase is associated with specific healing properties.

6. Astrological Associations:

- Some celestial events, such as meteor showers, comets, and specific star alignments, are believed to enhance the potency of bush medicine. These celestial occurrences are thought to bring about unique healing energies that can be harnessed during specific rituals.

7. Connection to Dreamtime Stories:

- Bush medicine practices are closely linked to Dreamtime stories. These stories often provide the cultural and spiritual context for the use of specific plants and their healing properties. The stories serve as a guide for understanding the connection between the spiritual and the physical world.

8. Rituals and Ceremonies:

- Celestial healing practices are intertwined with rituals and ceremonies that involve singing, dancing, and the use of specific instruments. These ceremonies are conducted under the guidance of elders and healers who possess the knowledge and spiritual connection needed for effective healing.

9. Holistic Healing:

- Aboriginal healing traditions encompass not only the physical but also the mental, emotional, and spiritual aspects of well-being. The use of bush medicine and celestial healing seeks to restore harmony and balance in the individual and their connection to the cosmos.

10. Modern Relevance:

- The use of bush medicine and celestial healing continues to be relevant in modern Aboriginal communities. Many individuals, even those living in urban areas, still practice and preserve these traditions as a way to maintain cultural identity and holistic health.

In conclusion, bush medicine and celestial healing are integral parts of the rich tapestry of Aboriginal Australian culture. The connection between the natural world, the celestial realm, and human health underscores the profound wisdom and spirituality of these ancient traditions. The use of native plants and the guidance of the stars and celestial events continue to offer healing, connection, and cultural continuity in Aboriginal communities.

Connecting with the Sky Ancestors: Astrological Birth Charts

In Aboriginal Australian astrology, the creation of astrological birth charts is a profound and spiritually significant practice. These birth charts, which are often referred to as celestial maps or sky connections, connect individuals with their ancestral past, the Dreamtime, and the broader cosmos. Here, we delve into the significance of astrological birth charts in Aboriginal astrology:

1. The Sky Ancestors:

- In Aboriginal belief, the Sky Ancestors are celestial beings who played a significant role in the creation of the world during the Dreamtime. These beings are associated with stars, constellations, and other celestial entities.

2. Dreamtime Connection:

- The Dreamtime is a central concept in Aboriginal culture, representing the period of creation when ancestral beings formed the land, plants, animals, and humans. Astrological birth charts provide a way for individuals to connect with this sacred time.

3. Birth Chart Creation:

- Astrological birth charts are created for individuals based on their birth date, time, and location. Each chart is unique and represents a snapshot of the cosmos at the moment of a person's birth.

4. Mapping the Cosmos:

- The birth chart is seen as a map of an individual's life journey. It is created by plotting the positions of celestial bodies such as the Sun, Moon, planets, and specific stars at the time of birth.

5. Sky Ancestors' Guidance:

- Aboriginal astrologers or elders who are skilled in interpreting celestial maps play a crucial role in connecting individuals with the guidance of the Sky Ancestors. They provide insights into an individual's life path and purpose.

6. Star Significance:

- Specific stars, constellations, and planetary positions are interpreted for their symbolic meanings. These interpretations help individuals understand their life's challenges, strengths, and potential.

7. Personal Identity:

- Birth charts are believed to offer insights into an individual's identity, purpose, and destiny. They help people understand their unique place within the grand design of the cosmos.

8. Cultural Continuity:

- The creation of astrological birth charts preserves and continues the rich cultural traditions and spirituality of Aboriginal communities. This practice is often passed down from one generation to the next.

9. Rituals and Ceremonies:

- Birth charts are often created during rituals or ceremonies led by elders and astrologers. These ceremonies may involve storytelling, dancing, and singing, connecting individuals to their cultural roots.

10. Relationship with the Land: - Birth charts also serve as a connection to the land and its sacred places. Aboriginal people believe that their place of birth is significant and is tied to their celestial path.

11. Modern Adaptation: - In contemporary Aboriginal communities, the creation of astrological birth charts remains relevant. It is a practice that helps individuals navigate the complexities of modern life while maintaining a strong connection to their ancestral wisdom.

12. Holistic Guidance: - Birth charts in Aboriginal astrology provide holistic guidance, including advice on health, relationships, and life decisions. They are a source of spiritual and practical wisdom.

13. Nurturing Relationships: - Birth charts can be used to understand and nurture relationships. They provide insights into compatibility and the cosmic connection between individuals.

In conclusion, astrological birth charts in Aboriginal Australian astrology offer a unique and profound connection to the cosmos, the Dreamtime, and the wisdom of the Sky Ancestors. They are a spiritual roadmap that guides individuals on their life journey, connecting them with their cultural heritage and the broader celestial realm. This practice highlights the deep spirituality and cultural continuity of Aboriginal communities and their enduring connection to the sky.

Skywatchers and Elders: Guardians of Celestial Wisdom

Skywatchers and Elders play a central and revered role in Aboriginal Australian astrology. Their wisdom, knowledge, and connection to the cosmos are integral to the spiritual and practical aspects of this ancient practice. In this discussion, we explore the significance of Skywatchers and Elders in Aboriginal astrology:

1. **Custodians of Cosmic Wisdom:**
    - Skywatchers and Elders are the custodians of a profound body of celestial knowledge passed down through generations. They have a deep understanding of the stars, planets, constellations, and their significance in Aboriginal cosmology.
2. **Guides to the Dreamtime:**
    - Elders, especially, are often considered as gatekeepers to the Dreamtime, the period of creation and spiritual ancestors. They interpret celestial events and their relation to Dreamtime stories and provide guidance based on these interpretations.
3. **Transmitters of Oral Traditions:**
    - Much of the celestial knowledge in Aboriginal culture is oral, and Elders are responsible for transmitting this wisdom. They share stories, songs, and rituals that revolve around the stars, ensuring the continuity of their cultural traditions.
4. **Stellar Navigation:**
    - Skywatchers have practical roles in the community as navigators. They use the stars and celestial landmarks to traverse the vast Australian landscape. Their celestial knowledge helps with journeys, hunting, and finding water sources.
5. **Cultural Significance:**
    - Elders and Skywatchers are highly respected within their communities. Their role extends beyond astrology; they serve as cultural leaders, educators, and keepers of traditions.
6. **Ceremonial Leaders:**
    - Both Elders and Skywatchers often lead or participate in celestial ceremonies and rituals. These events are crucial for strengthening the spiritual connection with the cosmos and ancestral beings.
7. **Interpreters of Signs:**
    - Skywatchers observe celestial phenomena such as meteor showers, eclipses, and the movement of planets. They interpret these signs for their communities, providing insights into future events or changes in weather patterns.
8. **Divination and Healing:**
    - Elders and Skywatchers may use celestial insights for divination or in the healing process. They look to the stars for guidance on personal and communal well-being.
9. **Storytellers and Educators:**
    - Elders and Skywatchers are gifted storytellers, using narratives to impart celestial knowledge. They educate younger generations, ensuring the survival of ancient wisdom.
10. **Stars as Ancestral Beings:**

- Skywatchers and Elders are intimately connected with the concept that stars are ancestral beings. They understand the relationship between humans, the land, and the cosmos, reinforcing this belief in the community.
11. **Maintaining Cultural Connection:**
    - In a changing world, Elders and Skywatchers play a vital role in maintaining the cultural and spiritual connection to the land and the skies. They ensure that the essence of Aboriginal astrology is not lost.
12. **Adaptation to Modern Life:**
    - While adhering to tradition, Skywatchers and Elders also adapt their knowledge to address contemporary challenges, such as land conservation and ecological issues.
13. **Bridge Between Generations:**
    - Elders and Skywatchers serve as a bridge between the wisdom of the past and the needs of the present. They pass on celestial knowledge to the younger generation, keeping the cultural flame alive.
14. **Consultation in Decision-Making:**
    - Communities often turn to their Skywatchers and Elders for advice on important decisions. They consider celestial guidance in areas like land management and community affairs.

In conclusion, Skywatchers and Elders are the guardians of Aboriginal Australian astrology, representing the enduring connection between their culture and the cosmos. Their roles extend to preserving tradition, interpreting celestial phenomena, providing guidance, and passing down the wisdom of the stars to future generations. Their contributions are fundamental to the spirituality, culture, and practical life of Aboriginal communities, affirming their significance in the contemporary world.

Seasons and Starlore: Agricultural Insights from the Skies

In Aboriginal Australian astrology, the connection between the seasons and celestial phenomena is of paramount importance. The relationship between the changing positions of stars, planets, and constellations and the agricultural practices of Aboriginal communities has been a part of their cultural and ecological wisdom for thousands of years. In this discussion, we delve into the intricate interplay between seasons and starlore in Aboriginal astrology:

1. **Lunar Calendar for Planting and Harvest:**
    - Aboriginal communities have developed lunar calendars that align with specific celestial events to determine optimal times for planting and harvesting. These calendars are based on the phases of the Moon and the positions of certain stars.
2. **Celestial Markers for Seasonal Change:**
    - Various stars and constellations serve as markers for the changing of seasons. For instance, the appearance of certain constellations can signal the beginning of a season for planting or hunting.
3. **Cosmic Synchronicity:**
    - The alignment of celestial events with seasonal changes is seen as a form of cosmic synchronicity. For instance, the rising of particular stars in the evening

sky may coincide with the onset of the wet season, indicating a time for planting.

4. **Dreamtime Stories and Seasonal Lessons:**
   - Dreamtime stories are interwoven with seasonal lessons. These stories often contain guidance on how to read celestial signs and predict changes in the natural world.
5. **Orion and the Coming of the Wet Season:**
   - The appearance of Orion in the night sky is a significant celestial event. Its rising is often associated with the approach of the wet season, signifying a time of abundance and growth.
6. **The Seven Sisters and Food Gathering:**
   - The Pleiades, known as the Seven Sisters, are essential in agriculture. Their appearance in the evening sky may indicate a time for collecting specific foods or engaging in hunting and gathering activities.
7. **Emu in the Sky and Migration of Birds:**
   - The Emu in the Sky constellation is closely linked to bird migration patterns. Aboriginal communities observe the Emu's movement to determine when certain birds will return, providing crucial information for hunting.
8. **Alignment of Stone Arrangements:**
   - Some stone arrangements found in Aboriginal lands are aligned with celestial events and seasons. These arrangements serve as calendars, helping communities keep track of seasonal changes.
9. **Ceremonies and Agricultural Rituals:**
   - Many Aboriginal ceremonies and rituals are directly tied to agricultural activities. These rituals involve celestial elements and are conducted to ensure a successful harvest.
10. **Connection to Country:**
    - The relationship between celestial bodies and the land is deeply ingrained in Aboriginal culture. The changing seasons are not merely practical considerations but a profound connection to the land, the Dreamtime, and the stars.
11. **Ecological Sustainability:**
    - Aboriginal practices of aligning agricultural activities with celestial events demonstrate their understanding of ecological sustainability. By closely observing the stars, they ensure the land is used judiciously.
12. **Adaptation to Climate Change:**
    - Aboriginal communities are increasingly incorporating their starlore with modern climate science to adapt to changing weather patterns. The knowledge of celestial markers helps them adjust planting and harvesting times.

In summary, the agricultural insights within Aboriginal Australian astrology are a testament to the deep connection between the celestial realm and the Earth. The wisdom of the stars informs the timing of agricultural activities, strengthening the bonds between Aboriginal communities, their ancestral lands, and the cosmos. This connection between seasons and starlore is not only practical but also a spiritual and ecological guide that has sustained Aboriginal cultures for generations.

Spirituality and the Stars: The Connection to Dreamtime

In the rich tapestry of Aboriginal Australian culture, the spiritual significance of the stars is deeply embedded in the Dreamtime, a sacred period in Aboriginal belief that encompasses the creation of the world, ancestral spirits, and timeless wisdom. Within this context, the celestial realm holds profound spiritual significance, offering a bridge between the earthly existence and the ancestral spirits. Let's explore the intricate connection between spirituality and the stars, as understood through the lens of Dreamtime in Aboriginal Australian astrology:

1. **Dreamtime Cosmogony:**
    - According to Aboriginal beliefs, during the Dreamtime, ancestral spirits created the land, animals, plants, and celestial bodies. The stars, planets, and constellations are seen as the remnants of these ancestral beings, representing their eternal presence in the cosmos.
2. **Celestial Ancestors:**
    - Aboriginal communities identify specific stars and constellations as the spirits of their ancestors. These celestial beings are revered and respected, and their movements in the night sky are considered messages from the Dreamtime.
3. **Starlore in Dreamtime Stories:**
    - Dreamtime stories often feature celestial elements, narrating the origins of stars, their relationships with Earth, and the lessons they offer. These stories are passed down through generations, connecting individuals to their spiritual heritage.
4. **Navigating the Dreamtime Sky:**
    - Aboriginal spiritual leaders, often called "Skywatchers" or "Stargazers," interpret the movements of stars to gain insights into the spiritual realm. They navigate the Dreamtime sky, guiding their communities in matters of spirituality, rituals, and ceremonies.
5. **Star Maps as Spiritual Guides:**
    - Certain star patterns serve as spiritual maps, guiding individuals in their spiritual journeys. For example, the Emu in the Sky constellation is considered a guide to the spirit world, helping shamans and seekers navigate the Dreamtime.
6. **Ceremonial Starlore:**
    - Ceremonial practices, including dances, rituals, and initiations, are conducted under specific celestial configurations. These ceremonies align with the movements of stars, enhancing their spiritual potency and connecting participants with the Dreamtime ancestors.
7. **Seasonal Rhythms and Spiritual Balance:**
    - Aboriginal spirituality emphasizes harmony and balance with nature. The changing positions of stars and celestial events mark spiritual milestones, reminding the community of the interconnectedness between Earth, the cosmos, and the spiritual realm.
8. **Dreaming Tracks:**
    - Dreaming Tracks, also known as Songlines, are ancient pathways that crisscross the land, connecting significant spiritual sites. These pathways are believed to have been created by ancestral spirits during the Dreamtime, and the stars above often mirror these terrestrial paths.
9. **Dreamtime Starlore Art:**

- Aboriginal art frequently depicts celestial motifs inspired by Dreamtime starlore. These artworks serve as spiritual expressions, reinforcing the connection between the artist, the Dreamtime, and the stars.
10. **Celestial Guidance in Spiritual Rituals:**
    - Spiritual rituals, including initiations, healings, and vision quests, are often conducted under specific celestial alignments. Aboriginal spiritual leaders interpret these celestial events to gain insights into the spiritual needs of individuals and communities.
11. **Eclipse Mythology:**
    - Solar and lunar eclipses are viewed as powerful spiritual events in Aboriginal culture. They are often associated with significant transformations and spiritual revelations, symbolizing the temporary merging of the Dreamtime with the present world.
12. **Personal Spiritual Journeys:**
    - Individuals often connect with their personal Dreamtime through stargazing and meditation. By aligning their spiritual practices with the stars, they seek guidance, protection, and communion with their ancestral spirits.

In essence, the spirituality of Aboriginal Australian astrology is intricately woven into the fabric of the Dreamtime. The stars are not merely distant cosmic entities but living beings with spiritual significance. Through Dreamtime starlore, Aboriginal communities find spiritual guidance, cultural identity, and a profound sense of belonging within the vast expanse of the celestial realm. The connection between spirituality and the stars in Aboriginal Australian astrology is a testament to the enduring wisdom of the Dreamtime, enriching the lives of individuals and communities across generations.

Weather Signs and Sky Predictions: Reading Nature's Signals

In Aboriginal Australian astrology, the study of weather signs and celestial predictions plays a crucial role in daily life and survival. Traditional knowledge passed down through generations allows Aboriginal communities to interpret signs from the sky and predict weather patterns. These insights are invaluable for hunting, gathering, ceremonies, and navigating the Australian landscape. Here, we delve into the significance of weather signs and sky predictions in Aboriginal Australian astrology:

1. Cloud Formations:

- Aboriginal communities closely observe cloud patterns, shapes, and colors. Different cloud formations can signal upcoming weather conditions. For example, dark, heavy clouds may indicate impending rain, while wispy, high-altitude clouds might foretell fine weather.

2. Star Clusters and Planetary Alignments:

- The positions of stars and planets in the night sky hold celestial clues to weather changes. Specific constellations and planetary alignments are associated with seasonal transitions and the arrival of weather patterns, like the monsoon.

3. Lunar Phases:

- The lunar cycle, particularly the phases of the moon, is closely monitored. Full moons can be associated with rain or flooding, while a crescent moon might signify dry and windy conditions.

4. Animal Behavior:

- Aboriginal astrology incorporates a profound understanding of the animal kingdom. Observing animal behavior is a significant component of predicting weather. For example, certain bird species may indicate the onset of rain by their calls or flocking behavior.

5. Wind Patterns:

- Aboriginal communities pay attention to the direction and strength of the wind. Particular wind patterns can provide information about incoming weather, such as strong winds from the west preceding a cold front.

6. Celestial Symbols:

- Indigenous Australians have a rich tradition of celestial symbolism. Certain star patterns, such as the Emu in the Sky, are associated with weather changes and are used as guides to predict rain or the arrival of particular seasonal conditions.

7. Firestick Signs:

- Firestick signs are often used to predict and manage wildfires, which are an essential aspect of land management for both safety and regeneration of the landscape. Specific celestial and weather conditions are taken into account before conducting controlled burns.

8. Moon Halos:

- A halo around the moon is considered a strong indicator of rain. This optical phenomenon is caused by the refraction of moonlight through ice crystals in the atmosphere, which may precede a change in weather.

9. Echoes of Dreamtime Lore:

- Weather predictions and interpretations are often intertwined with Dreamtime stories and cultural lore. Aboriginal astrology draws from the wisdom and teachings of ancestral spirits and Dreamtime narratives.

10. Climate Variability: - Aboriginal Australians have a deep understanding of the climate variability in different regions. This knowledge is critical for planning activities like farming, hunting, and water resource management.

11. Role in Ceremonies: - Weather predictions are integral to ceremonial planning. Timing ceremonies based on celestial and weather predictions ensures that they align with the natural order of things.

12. Community Knowledge Sharing: - The knowledge of weather signs and sky predictions is typically passed down through oral traditions, ensuring the continuity of this essential aspect of Aboriginal Australian astrology.

13. Rainmakers and Weather Specialists: - Some individuals within Aboriginal communities hold the role of rainmakers or weather specialists. They are responsible for monitoring celestial signs and performing rituals to bring rain during droughts or to mitigate excessive rainfall.

14. Contemporary Applications: - While modern meteorology has gained prominence, traditional Aboriginal weather prediction methods are still valued and are sometimes used alongside conventional forecasting for more accurate results.

Weather signs and sky predictions in Aboriginal Australian astrology are a testament to the profound connection between Indigenous communities and the natural world. They highlight the holistic approach to understanding and interacting with the environment and serve as a reminder of the significance of ancestral knowledge in navigating the Australian landscape.

Star Stories from Different Regions: Diverse Cultural Insights

Aboriginal Australian astrology is rich in celestial narratives and star stories that vary across different regions and Indigenous cultures. These star stories are deeply intertwined with the Dreamtime lore and the cosmology of each Aboriginal group, reflecting their unique connection to the night sky. Here, we explore a few star stories from different regions in Aboriginal Australian astrology:

1. The Emu in the Sky:

- The Emu in the Sky is one of the most famous star stories and is shared by several Aboriginal groups across Australia. The dark rift of the Milky Way is seen as the body of the emu, and the Coalsack Nebula represents the head. The Emu in the Sky's rising and setting are associated with the emu's movements in search of food and the changing seasons. This celestial emu is often used for practical purposes, such as tracking seasonal changes for hunting and gathering.

2. Orion's Belt:

- In some Aboriginal cultures, the three bright stars that form Orion's Belt are known as the "Three Brothers" or "Three Young Men." These stars have various roles in different Dreamtime narratives, often symbolizing a group of young men traveling together. The positioning and appearance of Orion's Belt can be used to indicate changes in the weather and the seasons.

3. The Seven Sisters:

- The Pleiades star cluster is known as the Seven Sisters in many Aboriginal cultures. This star cluster has its own Dreamtime story, where seven sisters are pursued by a man represented by the star Aldebaran. The rising and setting of the Pleiades are connected to seasonal changes, and their appearance in the sky marks the time for specific cultural activities, such as ceremonies and rituals.

4. The Morning Star and Evening Star:

- Venus, as the Morning Star and Evening Star, plays a significant role in Aboriginal Australian astrology. Depending on its position in the morning or evening sky, Venus can be seen as an ancestral spirit or a guide. Its appearance and movements often have connections to important ceremonies and cultural events.

5. The Southern Cross and the Pointers:

- The Southern Cross (Crux) and the two Pointer stars (Alpha and Beta Centauri) are prominent features in the southern hemisphere's night sky. Different Aboriginal groups have various interpretations of these stars. For some, they represent ancestral figures or totems. The Southern Cross, in particular, is often used as a directional guide for navigation.

6. Dark Constellations:

- Some Aboriginal cultures recognize dark constellations, which are formed by the dark spaces between the stars rather than the stars themselves. These dark constellations are equally significant in their narratives and are believed to influence events on Earth.

7. The Star-Map of Water Country:

- In the Torres Strait Islands, the night sky serves as a star-map of the surrounding waters. The positions and appearances of stars guide traditional sea navigation and fishing practices. Each star has a story associated with it, connecting the people to the sea and their ancestors.

8. The Cosmic Rainbow Serpent:

- The Rainbow Serpent is a fundamental concept in Aboriginal mythology. While it is more associated with Earth than with stars, its influence extends to the cosmos. Some Aboriginal groups relate the Rainbow Serpent to celestial bodies and their movements, emphasizing the interconnectedness of all aspects of creation.

These star stories and celestial narratives are integral to the cultural identity and spiritual beliefs of Aboriginal Australians. They serve as a reminder of the deep connection between Indigenous peoples and the natural world, providing guidance for practical purposes, as well as a profound spiritual and cultural framework. Each region's unique interpretation of the night sky contributes to the rich tapestry of Aboriginal Australian astrology.

Sky Art: Rock Engravings, Wandjina and Petroglyphs

Aboriginal Australian cultures have a deep and profound connection to the cosmos, which is expressed through various forms of art and storytelling. One of the most fascinating aspects of this connection is their use of rock engravings and petroglyphs to depict celestial narratives and mythological figures. The Wandjina, in particular, is a significant example of this practice.

1. The Wandjina Figures:

- Wandjina figures are iconic depictions of ancestral spirits in Aboriginal Australian cultures, particularly among the Worora, Ngarinyin, and Wunambal peoples of the Kimberley region in Western Australia. These figures are often depicted with large, round heads and minimal facial features. Their large eyes are a distinctive element and are sometimes interpreted as representations of stars, emphasizing their celestial connection.

2. Celestial Connection:

- Wandjina figures are believed to have created both the landscape and human beings. Their association with the celestial realm is integral to this creation story. According to Aboriginal lore, the Wandjina spirits came from the sky, bringing the Dreamtime stories and laws with them. This cosmic connection is mirrored in the art of the region.

3. Depicting the Dreaming:

- Wandjina figures are frequently represented in rock art as part of the Dreaming stories. These rock engravings serve as a form of documentation, preserving the cultural knowledge and stories of the Dreamtime for future generations. The art reflects the belief that the cosmos and the land are intertwined and that the celestial realm plays a vital role in the creation of life on Earth.

4. Star Maps and Celestial Events:

- Some rock engravings and petroglyphs incorporate elements that resemble star maps or celestial events. Certain arrangements of figures in the art have been interpreted as constellations or representations of celestial bodies, highlighting the significance of the night sky in Aboriginal culture. This is particularly evident in the Wandjina figures, which are often associated with rain and water, critical elements in a region subject to seasonal flooding and drought.

5. Ritual and Ceremony:

- The Wandjina figures are part of a broader cultural and spiritual system, often tied to rituals and ceremonies that involve celestial observation. For instance, the appearance of specific stars and constellations signaled the time for particular activities, such as initiation ceremonies. The rock engravings and petroglyphs may serve as instructional aids for these rituals.

6. Preservation and Protection:

- Many of these rock engravings and petroglyphs have been well-preserved due to their remote locations and the durable materials used. The cultural significance of these sites has led to efforts to protect and conserve them for future generations. In some cases, they are considered sacred sites, and access may be restricted to prevent vandalism and damage.

7. Cultural Continuity:

- The depictions of celestial beings like the Wandjina continue to be created and maintained by Aboriginal artists and knowledge holders. This practice ensures the transmission of cultural knowledge and maintains a strong connection between contemporary Aboriginal communities and their ancient celestial heritage.

In conclusion, the use of rock engravings and petroglyphs, including the iconic Wandjina figures, in Aboriginal Australian art underscores the deep connection between Indigenous cultures and the cosmos. These artworks serve as a visual and symbolic representation of the Dreamtime stories, the creation of the land, and the ongoing relationship between the celestial realm and the people. They are not only artistic expressions but also repositories of cultural knowledge and spiritual significance for Aboriginal communities.

The Role of Women in Aboriginal Australian Astrology

Aboriginal Australian astrology is deeply entwined with cultural, spiritual, and social practices that emphasize the interconnectedness of all aspects of life. Within this framework, women play essential roles in preserving, transmitting, and participating in astrological traditions. Here, we will explore the significant roles that women hold in Aboriginal Australian astrology:

1. Custodians of Cultural Knowledge:

- Women often serve as custodians of cultural knowledge, including astrological wisdom. They play a vital role in passing down stories, rituals, and celestial narratives to younger generations. Elders, particularly female elders, are instrumental in ensuring the continuity of oral traditions and preserving the wisdom of the Dreamtime.

2. Storytellers and Educators:

- Women are central to the practice of storytelling and education in Aboriginal communities. They are responsible for teaching the young about the Dreamtime, celestial beings, and the meaning of celestial events. Through their storytelling, women pass on not only astrological knowledge but also the cultural and spiritual significance of the stars.

3. Connection to Lunar Phases:

- Many Aboriginal communities follow lunar calendars for various activities, including hunting, gathering, and ceremonies. Women are intimately linked to lunar phases, as their menstrual cycles often align with the moon's cycles. This connection is seen as a source of power and wisdom, allowing women to understand the ebb and flow of life, much like the tides influenced by the moon.

4. Ceremonial Leaders:

- Women frequently take on leadership roles in celestial and other ceremonies. These rituals often involve the moon and stars, and women are responsible for organizing and conducting them. The timing of these ceremonies often depends on celestial events, such as the appearance of specific constellations.

5. Healing and Astrological Medicine:

- Traditional healing and astrological medicine are closely linked in Aboriginal cultures. Women who are healers, or "ngangkari," use their knowledge of the stars, moon phases, and celestial events to provide healing and well-being services. Their understanding of celestial influences on the human body and spirit is central to their healing practices.

6. Connection to Star Ancestors:

- Women are revered as carriers of the lineage and the connection to ancestral spirits. Their roles in birth and nurturing are seen as mirrors of the creative forces in the Dreamtime. In some communities, women are believed to be the earthly counterparts of celestial beings.

7. Lunar-Based Ceremonies:

- Women often lead or participate in lunar-based ceremonies that celebrate the phases of the moon. These ceremonies align with specific celestial events, such as the appearance of particular stars and constellations. They may involve singing, dancing, and storytelling under the night sky.

8. Birth and Rites of Passage:

- Women are central to birth ceremonies and rites of passage. Astrological insights may guide the timing of these events. For instance, the appearance of certain constellations can be significant in determining a child's totem or spiritual connection.

9. Protecting Cultural Sites:

- Women often play roles in protecting and conserving cultural sites, including rock engravings and petroglyphs, which contain celestial depictions. Their efforts are essential in ensuring that these sites remain intact for future generations.

10. Contemporary Practitioners:

- Many women continue to practice and engage with traditional astrological knowledge in contemporary Aboriginal communities. They hold a profound understanding of the significance of the stars, moon, and planets in guiding daily life and spirituality.

In Aboriginal Australian astrology, the roles of women are diverse and fundamental, reflecting their unique connections to the cosmos, lunar cycles, and ancestral wisdom. Women contribute significantly to the preservation and continuation of astrological traditions, serving as storytellers, educators, healers, and custodians of cultural knowledge in their communities. Their roles are pivotal in maintaining the cultural and spiritual fabric of Aboriginal societies.

Conclusion: Embracing the Cosmic Wisdom of Aboriginal Australian Astrology

Aboriginal Australian astrology, deeply rooted in the Dreamtime and the rich tapestry of indigenous cultures, offers profound insights into the interconnection of the celestial and earthly realms. As we conclude our journey through the celestial landscape of Aboriginal Australian astrology, it becomes evident that embracing this cosmic wisdom holds immense value for individuals and humanity as a whole.

Cultural Preservation and Resilience:

- Aboriginal Australian astrology is a testament to the enduring strength and resilience of indigenous cultures. It emphasizes the importance of preserving ancient traditions and the wealth of knowledge contained within them. By embracing and respecting these traditions, we honor the resilience of Aboriginal communities and their enduring connection to the land and sky.

Interconnectedness and Oneness:

- Aboriginal Australian astrology underscores the concept of interconnectedness—how all living beings, the land, and celestial bodies are intricately linked. This cosmic wisdom teaches us to perceive ourselves as part of a greater whole, fostering a sense of unity with the natural world and the cosmos. By embracing this perspective, we can strive for a more harmonious coexistence with the planet and its inhabitants.

Cultural and Environmental Conservation:

- The wisdom of Aboriginal Australian astrology draws attention to the importance of preserving not only cultural heritage but also the environment. The sacredness of the land and the celestial bodies calls us to be stewards of the Earth, advocating for the conservation of both natural landscapes and cultural sites. By recognizing the spiritual significance of the land and the stars, we can work to protect these treasures for future generations.

Spiritual Connection and Well-Being:

- The cosmic wisdom of Aboriginal Australian astrology provides a unique lens through which we can view our own spiritual connection to the universe. By immersing ourselves in the teachings of the Dreamtime and the starry sky, we can tap into a deeper understanding of our own spiritual essence. This connection can lead to a greater sense of inner peace, well-being, and purpose.

Holistic Healing and Medicine:

- The celestial healing traditions within Aboriginal Australian astrology invite us to explore holistic approaches to well-being. By integrating the wisdom of the stars, moon phases, and celestial events into our understanding of health and healing, we can embrace alternative and complementary practices that promote both physical and spiritual wellness.

Cultural Exchange and Reconciliation:

- Embracing the cosmic wisdom of Aboriginal Australian astrology invites us to engage in cultural exchange and reconciliation efforts. By respecting and learning from indigenous cultures, we foster a sense of unity and shared wisdom. We are encouraged to listen to and learn from the stories and insights of Aboriginal communities, nurturing a harmonious relationship between diverse cultures.

Cosmic Reverence:

- Finally, embracing the cosmic wisdom of Aboriginal Australian astrology encourages us to look up at the night sky with a profound sense of reverence. The stars and constellations above become not only objects of beauty but also carriers of ancient stories and cultural significance. By gazing at the stars, we connect with a living tradition that has spanned tens of thousands of years.

In conclusion, embracing the cosmic wisdom of Aboriginal Australian astrology offers us a unique opportunity to reconnect with our roots as humans—our shared origins in stardust and our connection to the Earth and the heavens. By honoring the Dreamtime, the stories of the stars, and the cultural traditions of indigenous communities, we enrich our lives with spiritual depth, cultural respect, and a renewed sense of interconnectedness in an increasingly fragmented world. This celestial wisdom is a gift, a bridge between the past and the future, and a testament to the enduring power of indigenous knowledge.

Made in the USA
Monee, IL
30 July 2025